SuperTots

3

Activity Book

PEARSON
Longman

Aleda Krause   Michelle Nagashima

Words and actions to the
SuperTots Theme Song

The magic that you need

(spread hands like stars and wiggle them beside ears)

Is there inside your head.

(point to head with both hands)

It's all you need to fly across the sky!

(spread arms and pretend to fly)

The world is wide,

(make circular motion with arms)

But you have it all inside.

(point to heart with both hands)

You're a SuperTot! You only have to try.

*(make fists and extend both arms straight up,
then wave them from side to side)*

Come on! Let's jump and run.
(beckon, then mime jumping and running)

We've only just begun.
(place hands on hips)

**Let's use our hearts and
all learn how to fly.**
(point to heart, then mime flying)

We'll laugh and have some fun,
*(make smile gesture next to mouth
with forefingers, then extend arms forward)*

Each and every one.
(point to different children)

You're a SuperTot! You only have to try.
*(make fists and extend both arms straight up,
then wave them from side to side)*

Find it!

 Find and circle furniture to match the furniture at the top. Color.

Number it!

All together

· ·

On your own

· ·

Listen. Find the picture. Write the number.

Unit 1 4

Sing it!

What's the difference?

Circle 5 differences. Color.

Cut and paste.

1

2

3

4

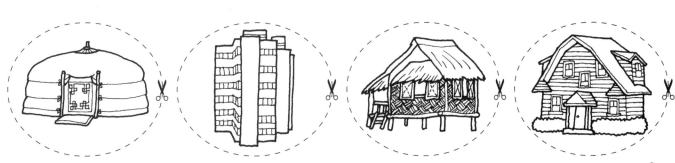

Cut out the homes. Paste them onto the pictures.

Picture Search A

All together

Listen. Color the B, S, and M at the top. Find items in the picture that begin with these letters. Color them the same color.

On your own

9 Unit 1

Listen. Color the T, P, and G at the top. Find items in the picture that begin with these letters. Color them the same color.

What is it? ??

Match it!

① ② ③ ④ ⑤

Match 4 of the 5 items at the top to the places. Match them to 4 of the 5 community helpers. Color.

Find it! Color it!

Find 10 rabbits. Color them.

princess

dragon

queen

king

wizard

crown

Color. Cut. Attach a stick.

Do it!

Number it!

All together

On your own

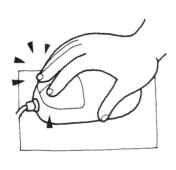

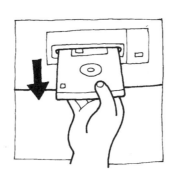

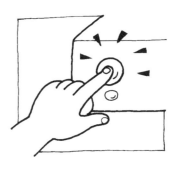

Listen. Find the picture. Write the number.

Picture Search A

All together

Listen. Color the F, H, and J at the top. Find items in the picture that begin with these letters. Color them the same color.

say it!
review Picture Search B

On your own ·

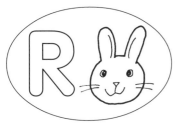  

Listen. Color the R, C, and D at the top. Find items in the picture that
begin with these letters. Color them the same color.

Shadow Match

① ② ③ ④ ⑤

Match the community helpers to their shadows. Color.

Number it!

All together

On your own

Listen. Find the picture. Write the number.

Follow the tracks.

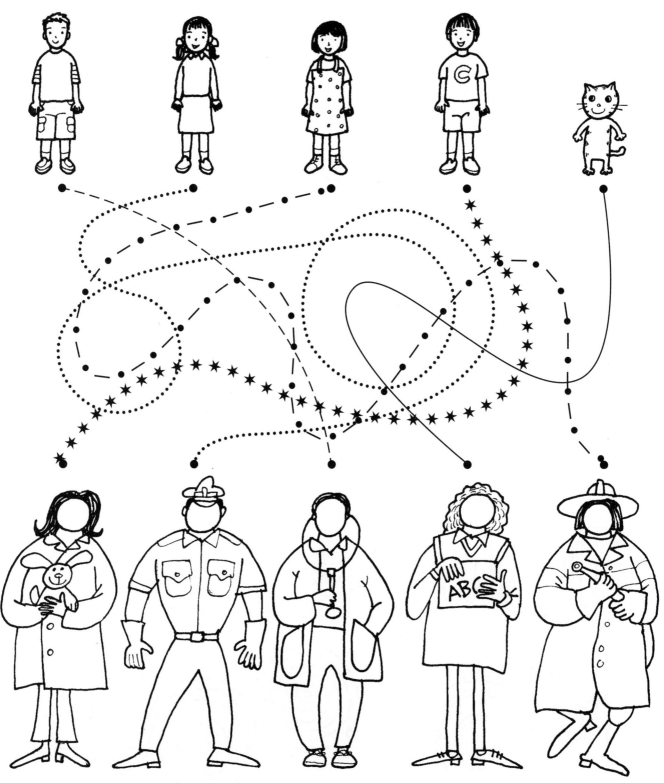

Color each child one color only. Follow the tracks. Color each community helper the same color.

 Discover it!

Cut and paste.

LIBRARY

SALE

Cut out the community helpers. Paste them onto the picture.

Say it!

Ii

Follow the path. 🔘

All together

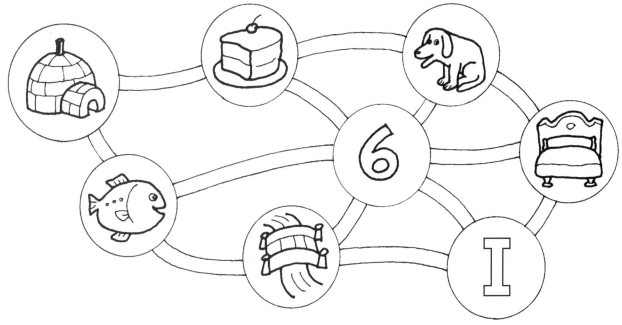

On your own

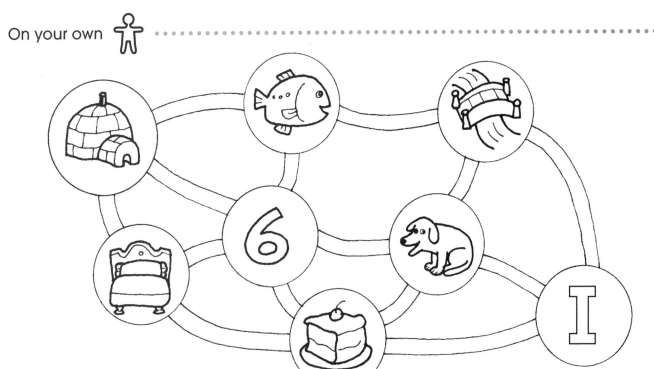

Listen. Follow the 'i' words from igloo to 'I'. Color.

What is it? ??

Listen and count it!

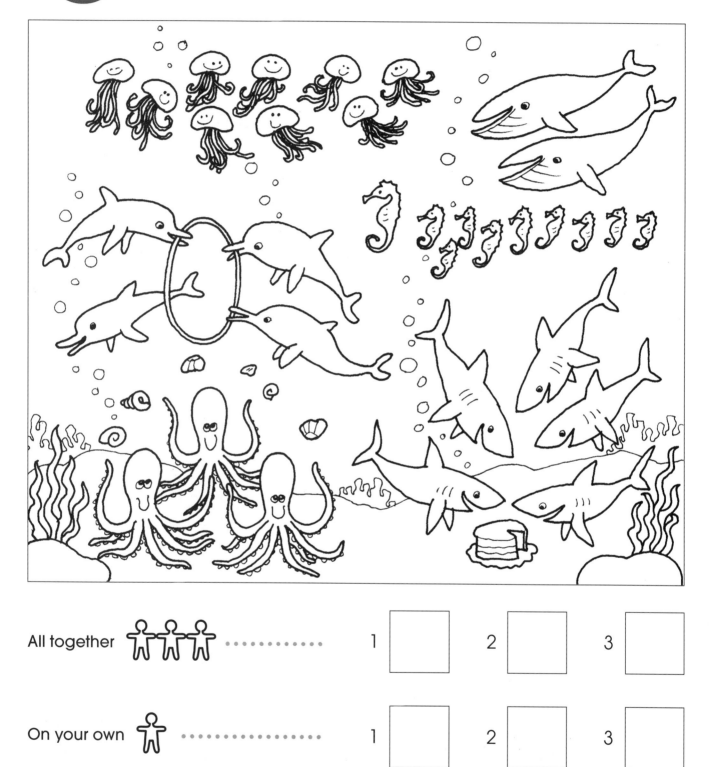

| All together | 1 | | 2 | | 3 | |
| On your own | 1 | | 2 | | 3 | |

Listen. Draw a circle. Count the sea creatures.

Draw it!

①

②

③

Draw different numbers of sea creatures into each box. Sing the How many jellyfish? Song with a friend and count the sea creatures.

Number it! 💿

All together  ···

On your own 🚶 ···

Listen. Find the picture. Write the number.

Cut and paste.

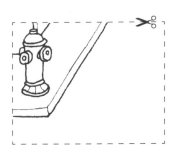
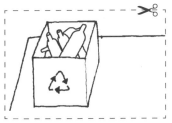
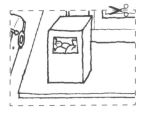

Cut out the pictures at the bottom. Paste them onto the scene.

Color. Cut. Put 2 sets together and play with a friend.

What is it?
??

Follow the pattern.

1

2

3

4

5

Choose 5 animals from the bottom. Draw them into the boxes above
to complete the picture paterns.

Circle it!

All together

① ✔ ✗

② ✔ ✗

③ ✔ ✗

On your own

① ✔ ✗

② ✔ ✗

③ ✔ ✗

Listen. Circle yes (✔), or no (✗).

 **Sing it!**

Cut and paste.

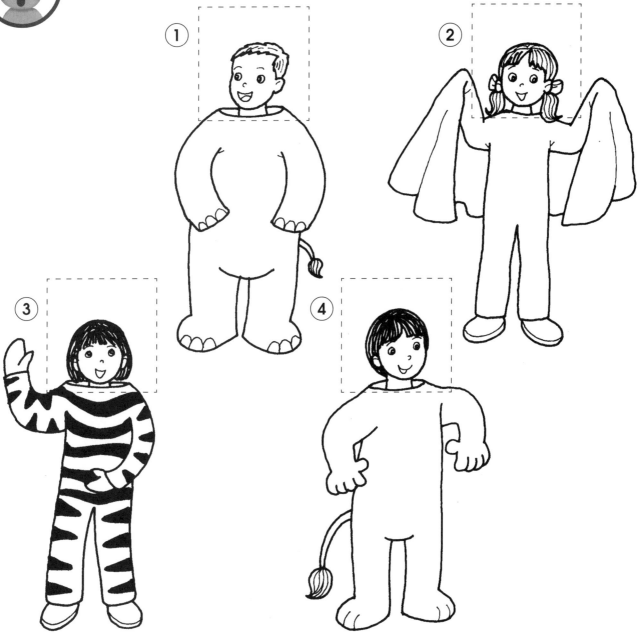

Cut out the animal masks. Paste 4 of the 5 masks onto the picture.

 **Match it!**

food

water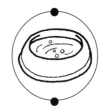

homes

Match the pets to 3 of the 4 types of food, water, and homes.
Match them to the children. Color.

Say it!

Follow the path.

All together

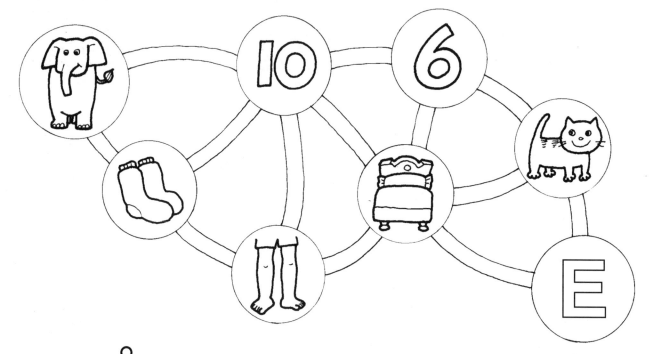

On your own

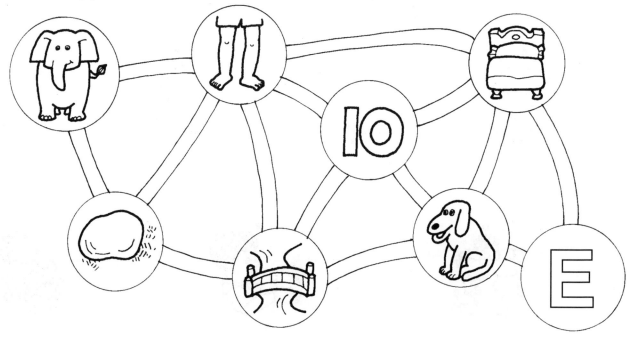

 Listen. Follow the 'e' words from elephant to 'E'. Color.

What's it like?

Story Strip

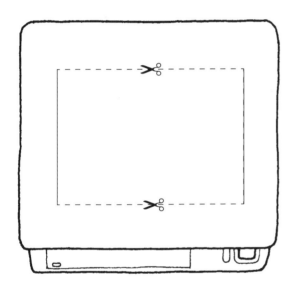

pull

Color and cut out the weather strip. Feed it through the computer screen. Practice the dialog.

Circle it!

All together

①  ✓ ✗

②  ✓ ✗

③ ✓ ✗

On your own

①  ✓ ✗

②  ✓ ✗

③  ✓ ✗

Listen. Circle yes (✓), or no (✗).

Sing it!

Color by number.

① 1 ② 2 ③ 3 ④ 4 ⑤ 5 ⑥ 6 ⑦ 7 ⑧ 8 ⑨ 9 ⑩ 10

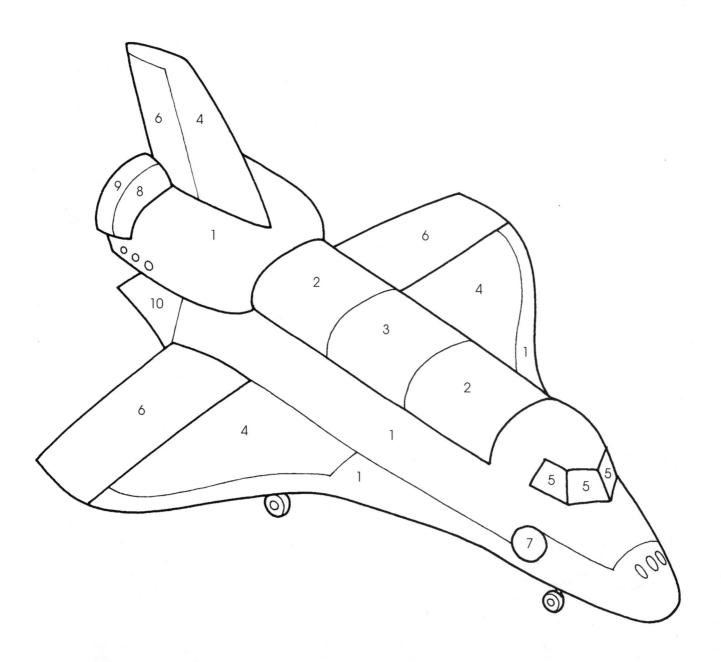

Color the numbers at the top a different color each. Color the picture.

Discover it!

Bingo

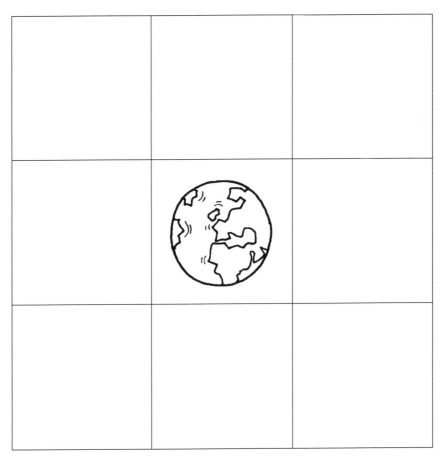

Color the items. Cut and paste them anywhere on the Bingo card.
Play Bingo.

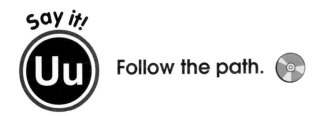

Say it!

Uu

Follow the path.

All together

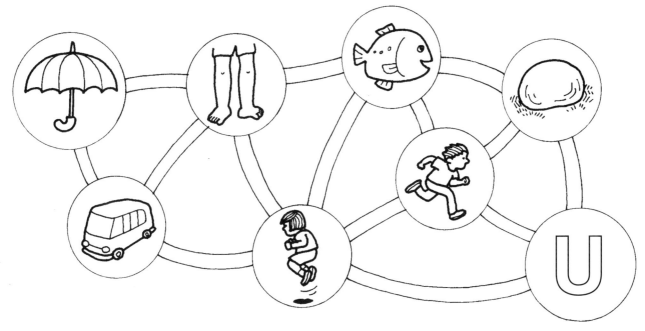

On your own

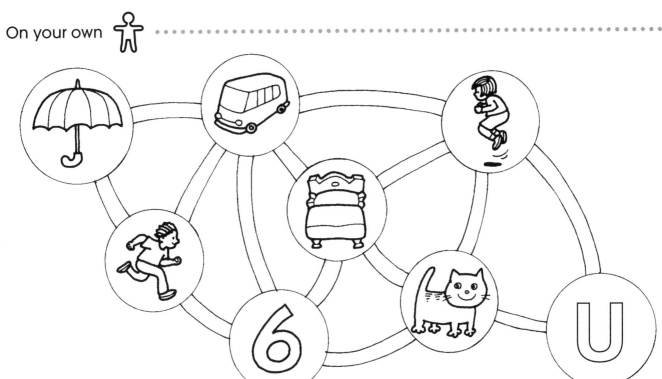

Listen. Follow the 'u' words from umbrella to 'U'. Color.

What is it?
??

Dot-to-dot

①

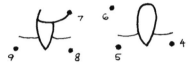

②

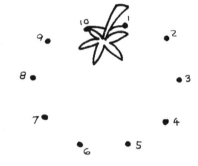

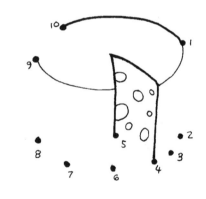

③

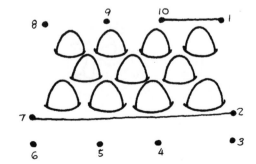

Connect the dots. Match items on the left to items on the right. Color.

Circle it!

All together

①  ✓ ✗

②  ✓ ✗

③  ✓ ✗

On your own

①  ✓ ✗

②  ✓ ✗

③  ✓ ✗

Listen. Circle yes (✓), or no (✗).

Find it! Color it!

Find things you can eat. Color them.

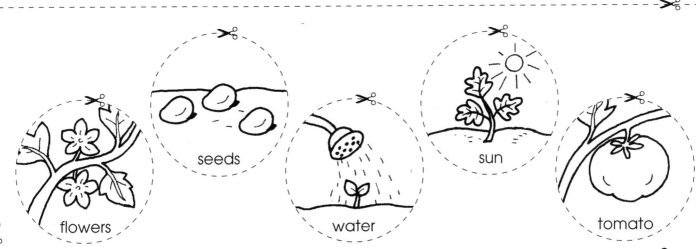

flowers | seeds | water | sun | tomato

Cut out the pictures. Listen. Paste them onto the circles.

Color. Cut. Put 2 sets together and play with a friend.

What is it?
??

Unit **8**

Science Experiment

item	Smooth	Slippery	rough
pebble	✓	X	X
soap			
rock			
bottle			

Test how the items feel. Check the boxes. Choose 3 more items and test them.

Do it!

Circle it!

All together  . . . .

①  ✓ ✗

②  ✓ ✗

③  ✓ ✗

On your own . . . .

①  ✓ ✗

②  ✓ ✗

③  ✓ ✗

Listen. Circle yes (✓), or no (✗).

What's the difference?

1

2

Circle 6 differences. Color.

Sing it!

Color and say.

Color. Practice the dialogs.

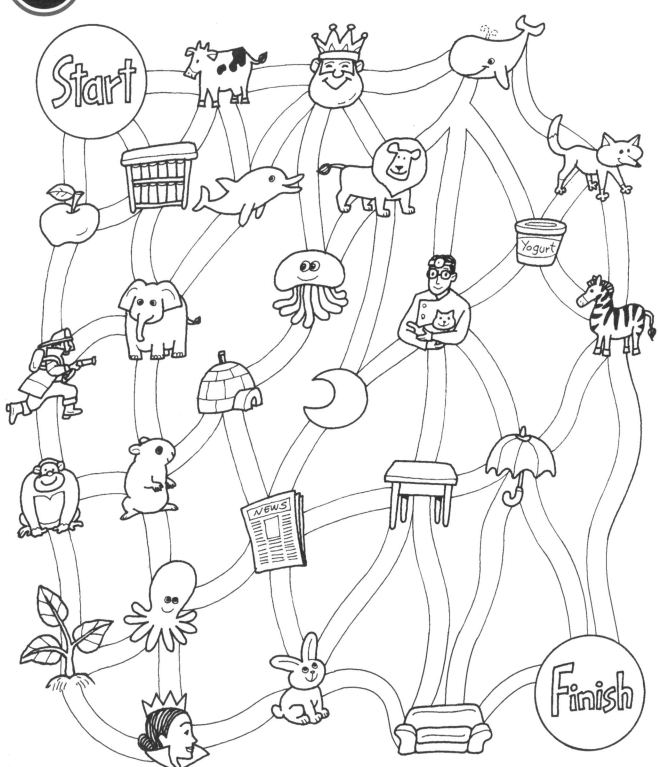

A B C D E F G H I J K L M N O P Q R S T U V W X Y Z

Follow the maze from 'a' to 'z' words.

General Instructions

Grandma's House

1. Color and cut out the inside and outside of the house and furniture.
2. Fold the house in half and glue the funiture into the rooms.
3. Cut along the dotted lines on the door and windows.
4. Fold the doors and windows open.

Animal Masks

1. Choose an animal. Enlarge the page to A3 size. Color the mouth, eyes, ears, and a paper plate.
2. Cut out the eyes, ears, and mouth and glue them to the plate.
3. Decorate the mask with colored paper.
4. Staple a strip of card to each side of the mask to make a headband.

Day Trip Mini Book

1. Color and cut out the template, the places, and the boy or girl.
2. Fold the template to make a mini book.
3. Glue the places into the pages of the mini book.
4. Tape the boy or girl to a chopstick.

Space Travel Craft

1. Color and cut out the background and the space items.
2. Attach the planet and glue the background to some card.
3. Cut a slit along the dotted line.
4. Use the tab to attach the astronaut to the shuttle. Tape the shuttle to a chopstick.

Community Helpers Flip Book

1. Color the pictures.
2. Cut out the pictures on the solid lines.
3. Glue the 4 pictures together on the shaded area to make a book.
4. Cut the book on the dotted lines.

Plant Life Craft

1. Color and cut out the movie strips and the flower.
2. Tape the movie strips together.
3. Cut along the dotted lines in the flower.
4. Feed the movie strip through the flower.

Octopus Craft

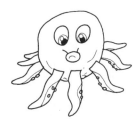

1. Use newspaper and scrunch it up to make the octopus body.
2. Cover it with crepe paper and tape it at the base.
3. Color and cut out the octopus eyes, mouth, and legs.
4. Tape them to the octopus body.

Tide Pool Craft

1. Color the inside base of a paper plate and the tide pool items.
2. Cut out and glue the tide pool items to the paper plate.
3. Cut out the base of a second paper plate.
4. Color the rim and tape the plates together.

Grandma's House

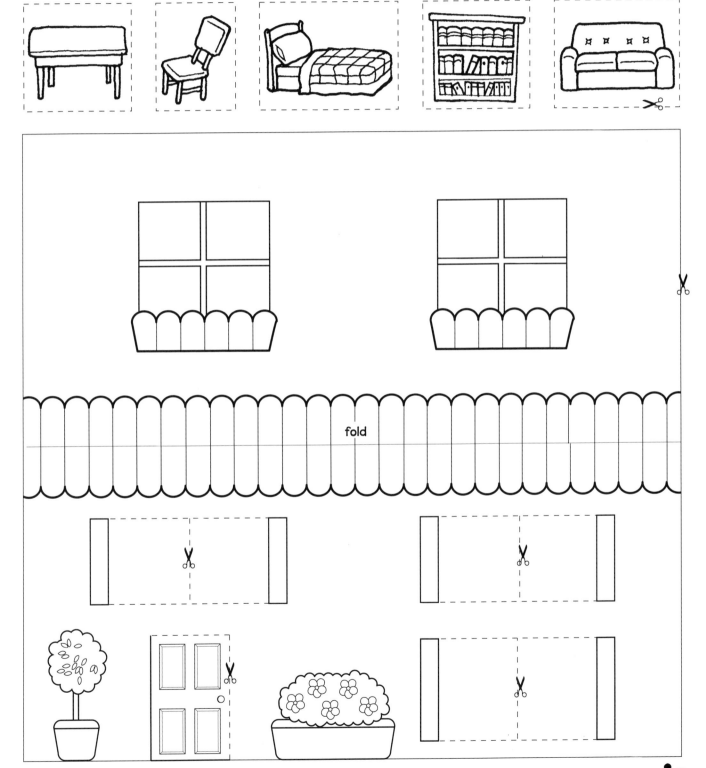

fold

Color. Cut. Make the house.

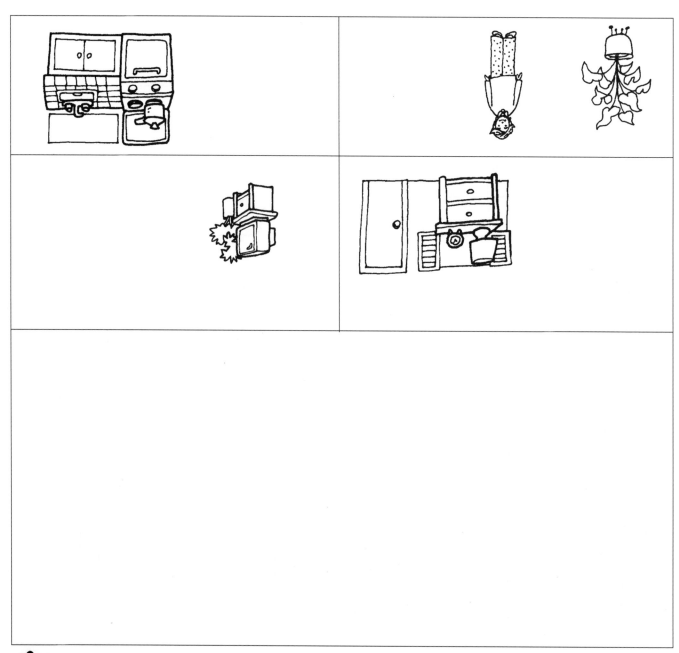

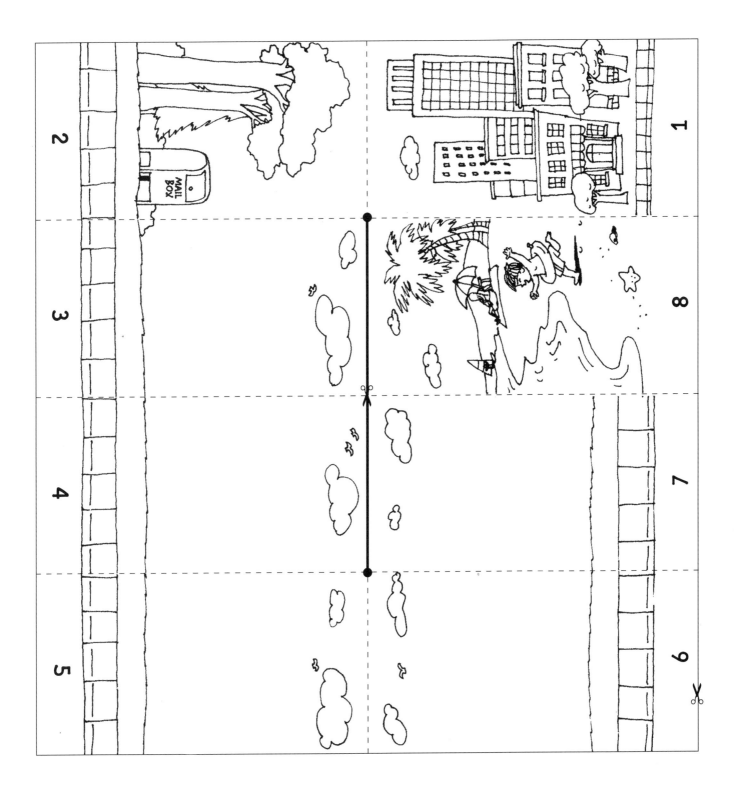

Color. Cut. Make the mini book.

 **Day Trip Mini Book 2**

zoo

museum

farm

library

park

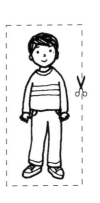

boy

girl

Community Helpers Flip Book 1

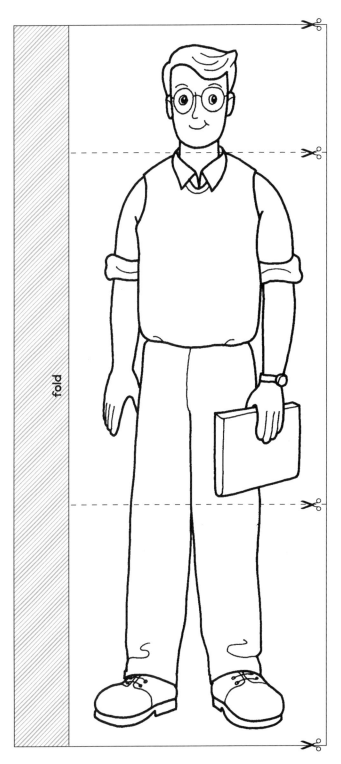

fold

fold

Color. Cut. Make the flip book.

Community Helpers Flip Book 2

fold

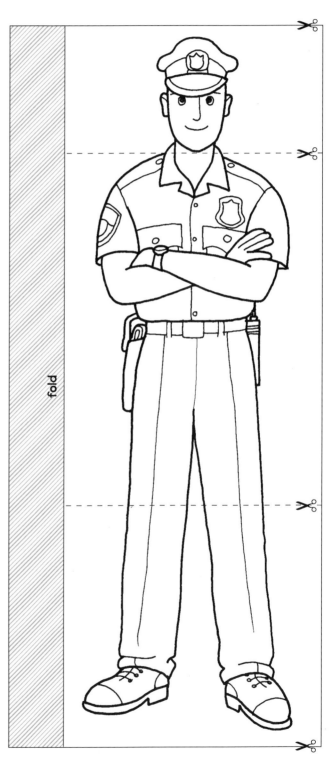

fold

Octopus Craft

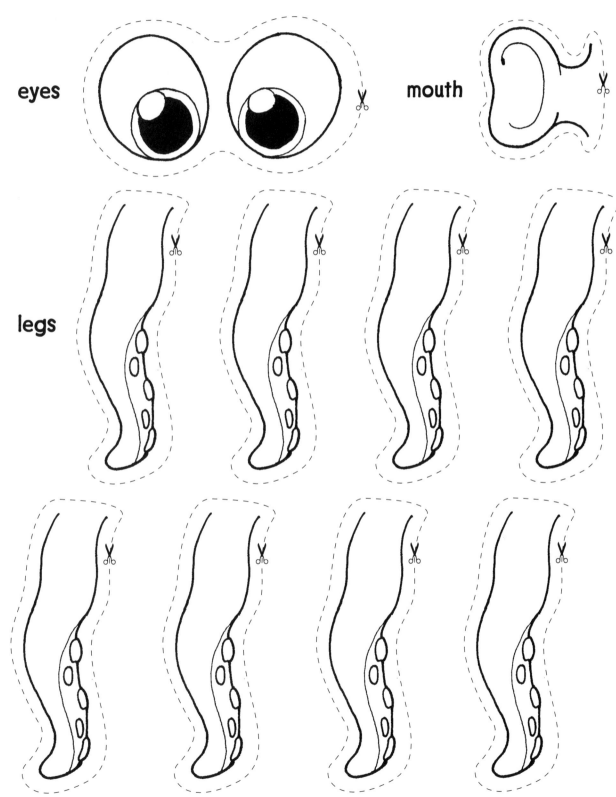

eyes

mouth

legs

Color. Cut. Make the craft.

Animal Masks 1

elephant

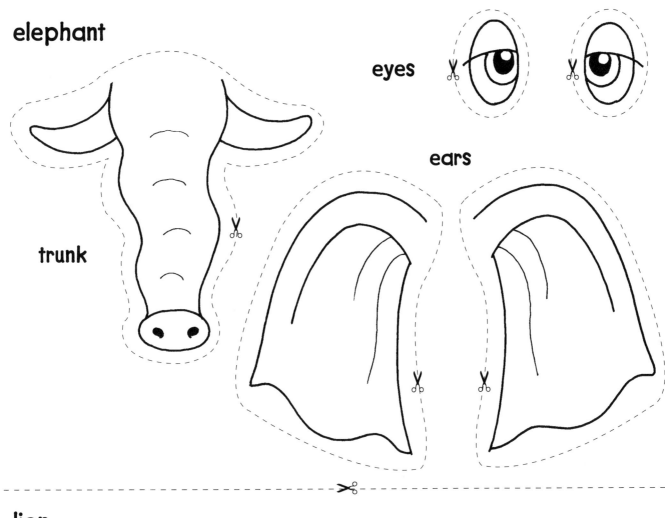

eyes

ears

trunk

lion

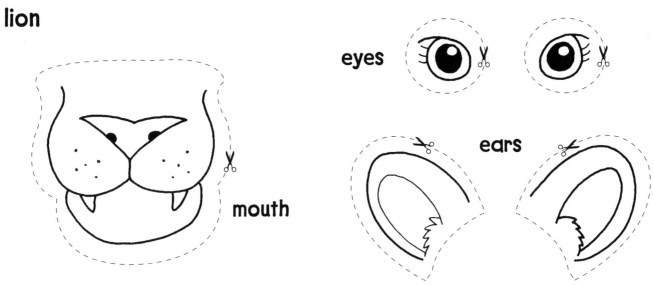

eyes

ears

mouth

Enlarge. Color. Cut. Make the masks.

 Animal Masks 2

gorilla

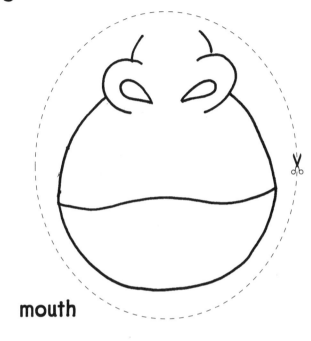

mouth

eyes

ears

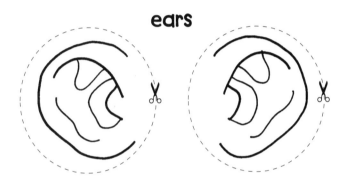

zebra

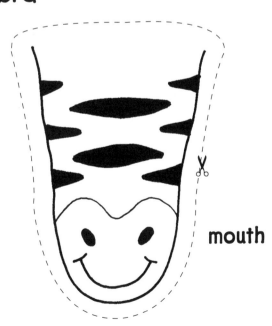

mouth

eyes

ears

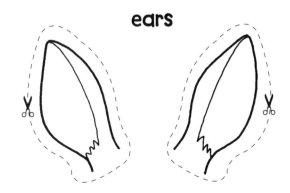

Space Travel Craft 1

fold

Space Travel Craft 2

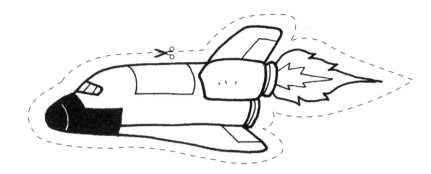

space shuttle

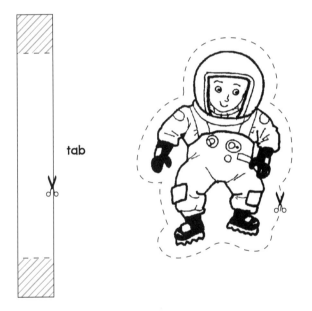

tab

astronaut

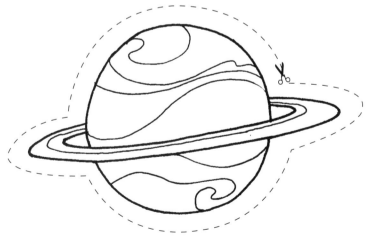

planet

Plant Life Craft

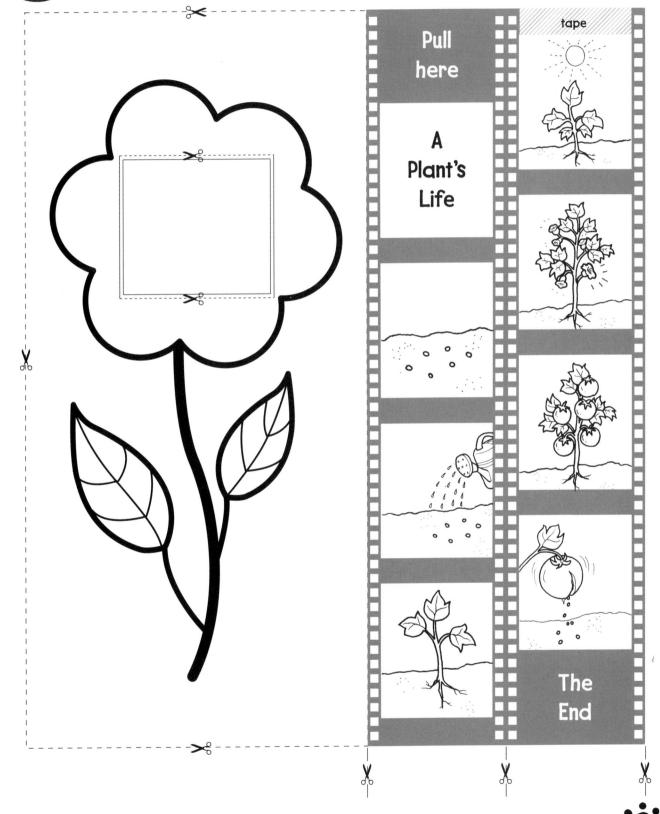

Pull here

A Plant's Life

tape

The End

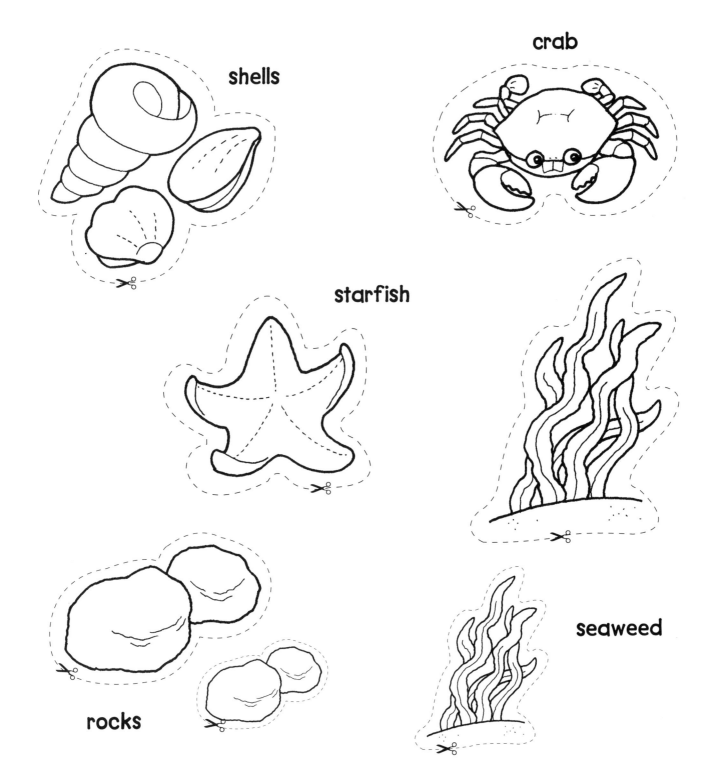

shells

crab

starfish

seaweed

rocks

Color. Cut. Make the craft.